Wheels

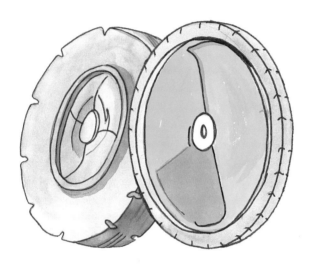

Illustrated by Karl Gunson

PEARSON

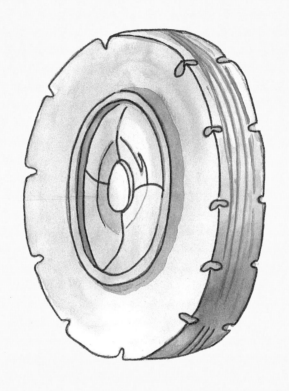

This is for
the car.

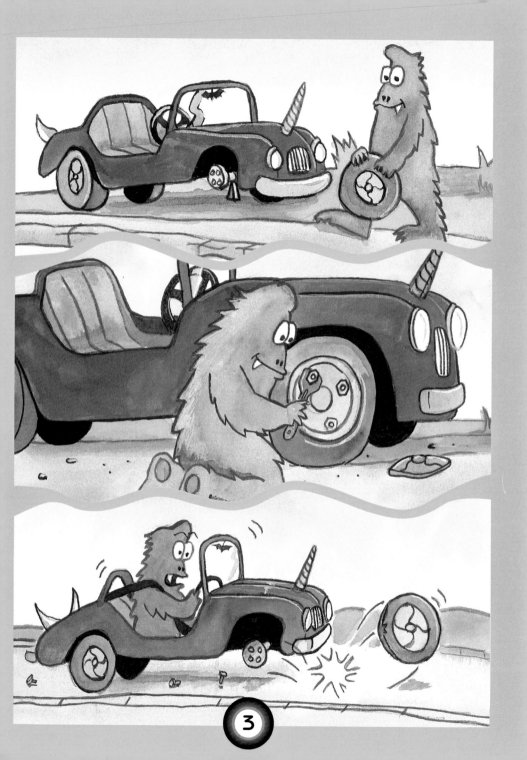

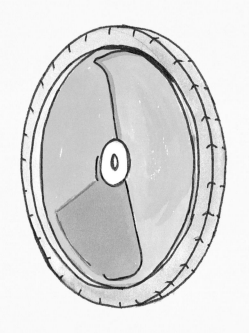

This is for
the bike.

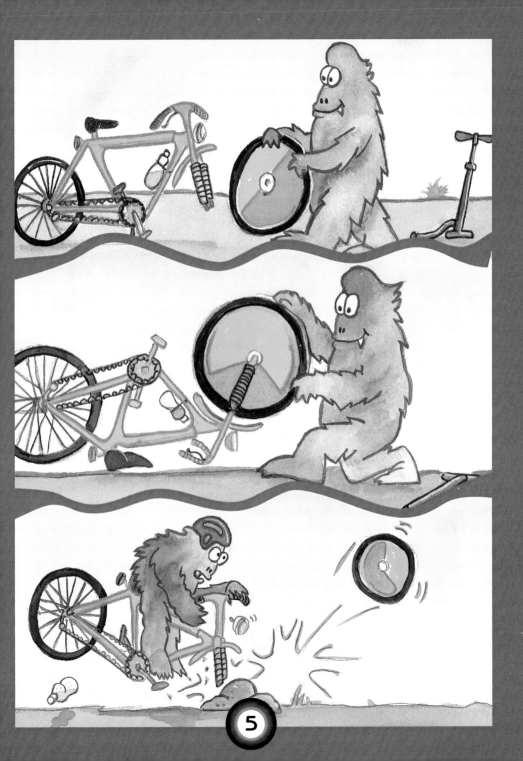

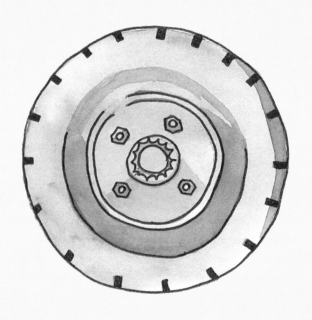

This is for
the bus.

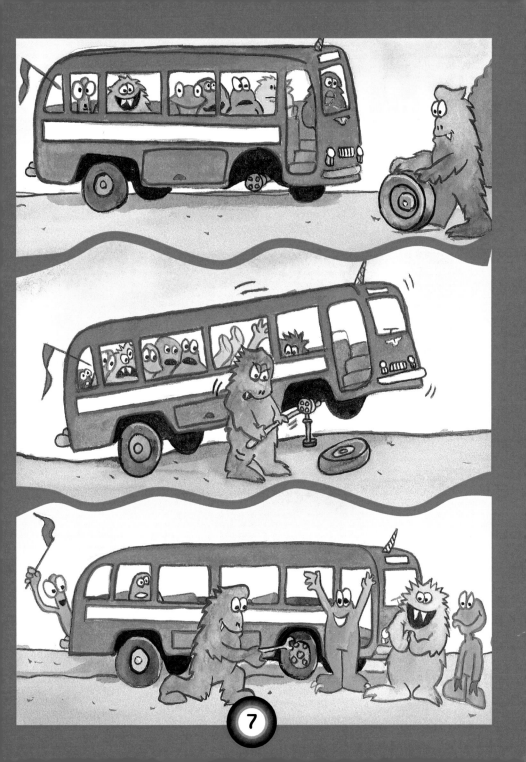

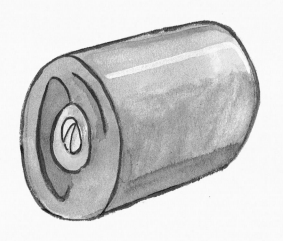

This is for
the skateboard.

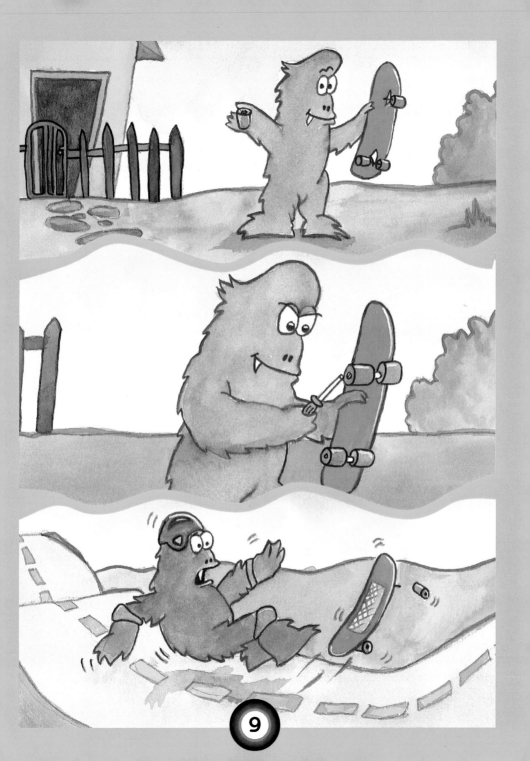

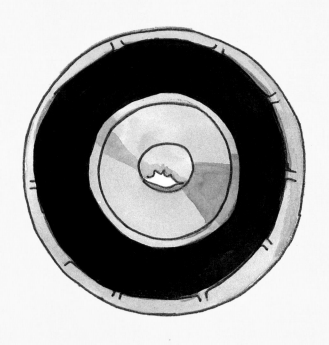

This is for
the truck.

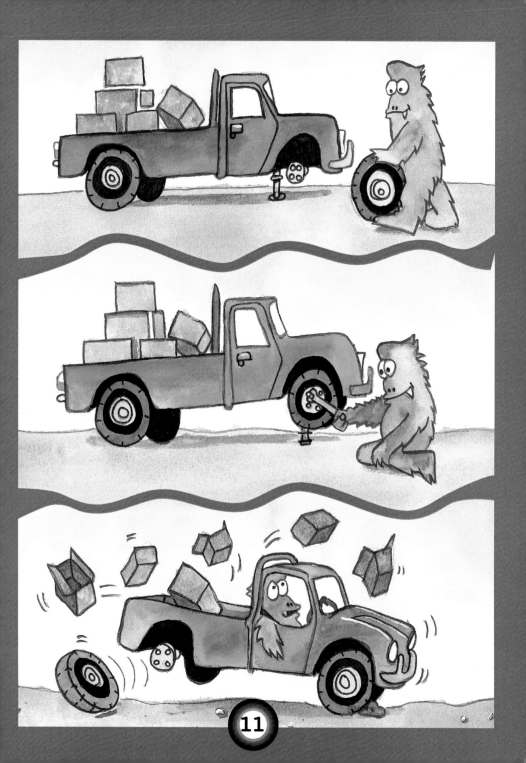

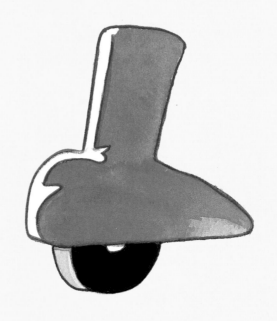

This is for
the plane.

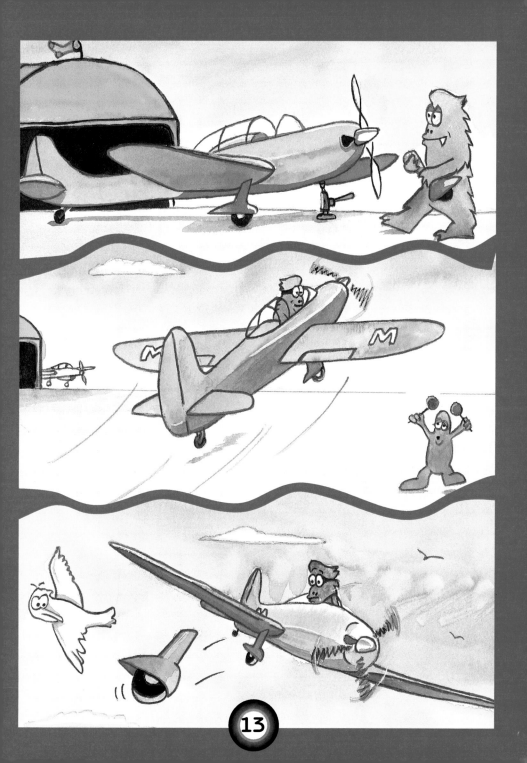

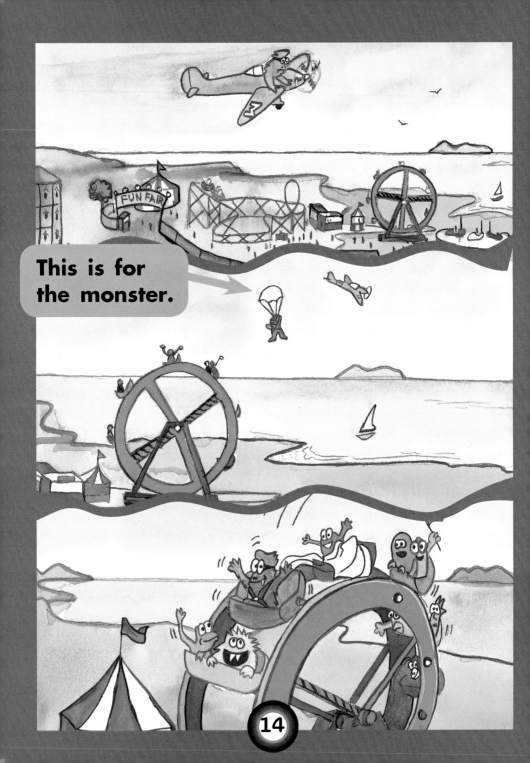

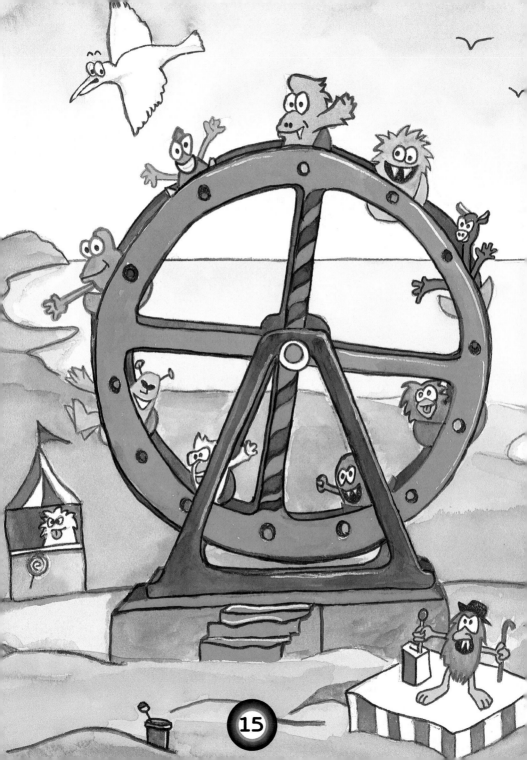

15

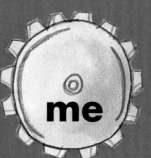
me

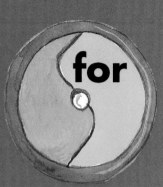
for

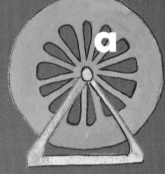
a

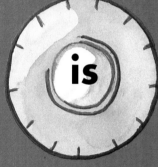
is

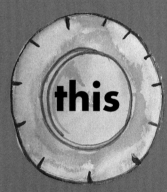
this

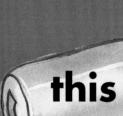
this

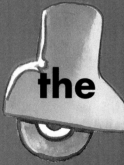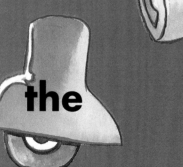
the

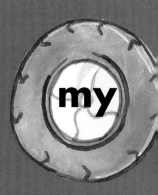
my